101

UNBELIEVABLE FACTS ABOUT RUNNING

THAT WILL MOTIVATE YOU TO GET UP AND RUN!

CONTENTS

CAUTION
RUNNERS

INTRODUCTION

If you have been thinking about starting running for some time, but haven't found a good reason to actually put on your sneakers and go, then this book is for you! After reading these 101 Unbelievable Facts About Running, you'll want to get up and start running immediately!

Before we get started on our 101 Unbelievable Facts About Running, let's start with a bit of common knowledge about running:

Running is the most natural way to move and exercise.

Running is the cheapest exercise to engage in.

Running requires almost no equipment or expensive gym memberships.

Running requires very little time and can be very effective. Even when done for 5 minutes!

Running is a natural ability that almost all species possess.

Running is good for your mind, body, and soul.

Running is eco-friendly as it only requires 2 legs.

Running can be practiced on your own, with friends and family, or even with your pet.

Running can be done in almost any terrain or environment.

Running can be done in silence or with background music.

Running is a personal experience that can be very calming and meditative.

Running fits into any lifestyle no matter if you are a CEO or a stay at home mom.

Yes, you.

No excuses.

You can run!

SURPRISING FACTS

- 1 -

Running burns about 50% more calories than walking.

For example, if you weigh 68 kg, you'll burn approximately 85 calories after 20 minutes of walking. Meanwhile, 20 minutes of running will burn approximately 225 calories.

- 2 -

The amount of calories you burn while running depends on your weight.

More weight you have, the more calories your body has to burn when running. The more weight you want to lose while running the longer and farther you will have to run for.

- 3 -

You run your fastest in your 20's.

Men are fastest at age 27, while women are at their peak running performance at the age of 29. Before that age, our speed increases each year. After that age, our speed starts to decrease.

- 4 -

Long distance running can be practiced well into your 90's.

There are many 90-year-olds that have completed marathons. Some have been running all of their life and some only started at the age of 89!

- 5 -

On average, men tend to be faster runners than women no matter the distance.

There are many reasons for this. First of all, higher levels of testosterone in men helps this a lot. Additionally, men's' hearts are 20-25 percent larger than a woman's heart, giving them better circulation and oxygen to carry on running faster and longer. Women are naturally predisposed to carrying more weight, which means that they have to run harder to achieve the same running capabilities as men.

- 6 -

You burn more calories running outdoors rather than indoors due to air resistance.

Races that take place outside factor in the Wind Assistance Phenomenon. This phenomenon can help or hurt a runner by adding or subtracting up to 2 meters per second when running.

- 7 -

The four fastest animals in the world are cheetahs, rabbits, kangaroos, and cats.

- 8 -

The four slowest animals in the world are elephants, squirrels, pigs, and snails.

- 9 -

1 billion pairs of running shoes are sold worldwide each year.

- 10 -

Running improves more than just your health.

Besides being great for staying healthy, running regularly has been shown to reduce stress and anxiety, improve concentration, strengthen learning abilities, and increases creativity.

-11-

Running has an impact on your sex drive.

Those who run regularly report having a more satisfying sex than those who don't engage in physical recreation often. it has been shown that regular runners have more sex and achieve orgasms more frequently as well.

-12-

Eating bare-root improves your running speed.

The nitrates present in this purple vegetable are thought to be the reason behind the improvements in a runner's speed.

-13-

Running short sessions rather than long distances is best for reaching your weight loss goals.

Running is an effective way to lose those extra pounds. Running short distances has the same effect as a cardio workout. Alternate sprinting with slow run and exercises for the maximum results.

- 14 -

Listening to music can boost your running speed by 15%.

For many runners, earplugs and a playlist are a must have when running. Choose music that makes you motivated and excited to run.

- 15 -

The oldest person on record to complete a marathon was 101 years old.

His name was Fauja Singh and he was 101 when he completed the London Marathon in 2012. He finished with a time of 7 hours 49 minutes and 21 seconds. Gladys Burrill was the oldest woman to complete a marathon at the age of 92.

- 16 -

Athletes who wear red clothing have more likely to win a race.

- 17 -

When women run, their breasts move up and down with the rhythm of their running. It is important for women to wear a supportive sports bra to minimize movement and avoid premature sagging of the breasts.

- 18 -

A woman's breasts can move around the same amount regardless of whether they are running fast or slow.

- 19 -

Wearing cheap running shoes could lower your risk of injury.

According to a research study at the University of Bern in Switzerland, it was found that runners who wore shoes that cost less than $40 were 2 times less likely to get injured as compared to those runners who wore shoes worth more than $40.

- 2 0 -

Stretching before a run might not always be a good idea.

Many runners couldn't imagine going on a run without stretching first. However, this routine could actually hinder your running performance. Research has shown that stretching right before a run can make the body less efficient, causing you to run slower. A good substitution for stretching would be to warm up with dynamic movements to prepare your muscles for exercise. This warm-up will also raise your heart rate and body temperature. Save your stretching for a cool down after a run or race.

- 21 -

Men who run regularly have higher chances of conceiving a daughter.

A study taken at the University of Glasgow found that men who ran more than 30 miles per week while trying to conceive rarely conceived male babies. This is due to the lower amounts of testosterone in men who run long distances. So, run longer regularly if you want to conceive a girl.

- 22 -

Running backward creates fantastic benefits.

It may be surprising to learn that by running backward, you train the muscles in your body to adapt to new forms of coordination. Runners who practice running backward are less likely to have injuries and perform better on a wide variety of terrains.

- 23 -

Human feet can produce up to ½ a liter of sweat per day.

You have probably never thought about it before, but our feet produce an incredible amount of sweat. Choose cotton socks to avoid the unpleasant odor and effects that can come from sweaty feet.

- 2 4 -

At regular points during a run, both of your feet are off the ground.

This phenomenon has been photographed during many races. It almost looks like the runners are flying! Pretty impressive, ha?

- 2 5 -

The taste of breastmilk can change after intense running sessions or training.

The taste of breastmilk can sour because of the lactic acid your body produces during strenuous exercise. So, don't be worried if your little one doesn't want to eat after your intensive running session.

- 2 6 -

Being short gives you an advantage when running.

Here is another amazing fact you didn't know about. Taller runners are no match for shorter ones because they have longer and heavier bones and need a lot more energy to move them around. Although they can have the same weight, it's difficult for a taller runner to match the speed and power of a shorter and lighter runner.

- 2 7 -

Runners will correct their posture and stand straighter when an attractive runner of the opposite sex is coming towards them.

- 2 8 -

The German Markus Jürgens holds the world record in marathon backward running. At the 2017 Hannover Marathon, he crossed the finish line with a time of 3 hours, 38 minutes, and 27 seconds.

- 2 9 -

Some runners guard their nipples against friction and chafing by wearing band-aids or rubbing Vaseline over them.

- 3 0 -

Before the 1960s it was believed that drinking water was harmful to running performance.

Doing so was strictly forbidden in races shorter than 10 miles in Europe and the United Kingdom.

- 31 -

When we run, our heart creates enough pressure to squirt blood 30 feet.

- 3 2 -

Running is more efficient in reducing your blood pressure than most pharmaceutical medications.

Medications and diets are not always as effective as we expect, and most of them have some side effects. With running, you can get the same, long-lasting results without the side effects that come from medications.

- 3 3 -

You have your mom's genes to thank for your running abilities.

It's no surprise that most of our natural talents come from our parents. Research has shown that the genes responsible for our fitness capabilities come from our mothers.

- 3 4 -

"Runner's High" is a real phenomenon, not just a phrase. Every committed runner has experienced it. The more you push yourself when running, the more addicted you become to the serotonin rush that fills your body when you run.

- 3 5 -

It takes 200 muscles to make a step when you run. That is why running is so efficient for exercising the whole body and burning the most amount of calories.

- 3 6 -

Running works out 26 bones, 33 joints, 112 ligaments, and numerous nerves and blood vessels. Just imagine how hard your body has to work to make you run.

- 3 7 -

While we all know that running makes you strong and healthy, many of us are not aware that it can also make you sick! Excessive running – distances of 80 kilometers or more in a week –

increases the risk of catching a cold, flu, or respiratory illness. The ideal length to run for strengthening the body and the immune system is around 20-30 km per week.

- 3 8 -

Run for three days and die.

This is something that most people don't know. The average untrained runner has enough energy stored in their body to continuously run for three days at a maximum speed of 24 kilometers per hour. Trying to attempt this will wear out not only your muscles but your heart as well and would likely lead to death.

- 3 9 -

Half a percent of the population of U.S. has completed a marathon.

- 4 0 -

On average, 104.3 calories are burned every mile when running at a pace of 10 minutes per mile.

- 41 -

The average finishing time for men in U.S. marathons is 4:26. The average finishing time for women in U.S. marathons is 4:52.

- 42 -

Men tend to reach their maximum running speed at the beginning of a race while women reach their maximum speed towards the second half of a race. This is due to how the heart rate increases differently in men and women.

- 43 -

Even the most powerful computers can't generate the number of computations it takes to run on two legs. Even though running seems like a simple activity, the truth is that it is an incredibly complicated process for the body to complete.

- 44 -

Humans are faster than almost every other animal on earth when it comes to running long distances.

- 4 5 -

Rosa Ruiz won the Boston Marathon in 1980. It was later discovered that she joined the race near the finish line. This wasn't her first time cheating at a race. Officials also discovered that she had taken a subway to the finish line in the 1979 New York City Marathon.

- 46 -

Have you ever wondered where the word 'marathon' came from? Legend has it that the Greeks defeated the Persians in battle in 490 BC. The soldier Pheidippides ran from Marathon, a place in Greece, to Athens to deliver the good news. When he arrived, he promptly died but not before he managed to shout, "Rejoice, we are victorious." They say that the distance he ran, 26.2 miles (42km), is the reason for the distance of a modern marathon.

- 47 -

The ancestors of humans had to hunt to survive. That's how they developed the ability to run long distances about 2.6 million years ago.

- 48 -

"Pedestrianism" was the name for running in the late 19th century.

- 4 9 -

Until the late 1960s, recreational running was not mainstream. In 1958, the Chicago Tribune wrote about a strange new fitness practice: jogging.

- 5 0 -

Bill Bowerman, Nike co-founder and University of Oregon running coach, introduced recreational running to the United States. He said it was in 1962 on his trip to New Zealand when he discovered the benefits of recreational running.

- 5 1 -

In 1967, Kathrine Switzer entered the Boston Marathon under the name K. V. Switzer. She did this so that officials would not recognize her as a woman and in doing so, became the first woman to run a marathon.

- 5 2 -

The first woman who completed the Boston Marathon in 1966 (with an unofficial time of

3:21:25) was Roberta Gibbs. She hid behind a bush and joined the marathon when it started. In 1972, the Boston Marathon became the first race that allowed women to officially enter.

- 5 3 -

Serge Girard, French ultramarathoner, holds the record for the longest distance ever run in a year. He ran a total length of 27,011 kilometers over the span of 25 European countries over the course of 1 year. Prior to Serge, the record was held by India's Tirtha Kumar Phani.   She completed 22,581.09 km in 365 days. That is an average of 61.87 km per day!

- 5 4 -

The fastest mile was run by Moroccan, Hicham El Guerrouj. In 1999, he ran the mile in 3:43:13. Interestingly enough, the second fastest record holder is the 2nd place winner of that same race.

- 5 5 -

Svetlana Masterkova holds the record for the fastest mile run by a woman. She set the record in 1996 by running a mile in 4:12:56!

- 5 6 -

The fastest marathon runner in the world is Kenyan Dennis Kimetto, who set the world record of 2:2:57 at the 2014 Berlin Marathon.

- 5 7 -

Paula Radcliffe ran a marathon in 2:15:25 during the 2003 London Marathon. That's the fastest marathon time for a woman.

- 5 8 -

Stefan Engels, the "Marathon Man", ran 365 marathons in 2011 at the age of 49. That's the record for the most marathons run in consecutive days.

- 5 9 -

The Jamaican sprinter Usain Bolt is the fastest runner in the world. He set the record for the fastest human foot speed. He holds the world record in the 100-meter dash (9.58 seconds) and the 200-meter dash (19.19 seconds). His maximum recorded speed is 44.72 km/h (27.8 mph).

- 6 0 -

There are 2.6 million Kenyans who practice the sport of naked night-running.

- 6 1 -

The treadmill was initially designed for English prisons as a tool for punishment. The writer Oscar Wilde was forced to run on a treadmill during his time in prison.

- 6 2 -

During a 10-mile run, feet strike the ground around 15,000 times, at a force of three to four times the body's weight.

- 6 3 -

The Badwater Ultramarathon claims to be the world's toughest footrace. Stretching 135 miles (217 km) from Death Valley (the lowest point in North America) to Mount Whitney (the highest point in the lower 48 states). This grueling race is by invitation only.

- 6 4 -

The largest U.S. running race is The Bay to Breakers in San Francisco, with over 100,000 participants a year.

- 6 5 -

The oldest marathon finisher is Fauja Singh from India. He completed the Toronto Waterfront Marathon in Canada when he was 101-year-old with a time of 8 hours, 25 minutes and 16 seconds.

- 6 6 -

The youngest marathon runner in the world had already finished 48 marathons before he turned five. His name is Budhia Singh.

- 6 7 -

In the 1960s, running for exercise was so unusual that police became suspicious if they saw a grown man running at night. Many people were often stopped so runners switched to going out in the morning rather than at night.

- 68 -

Although proper running shoes are good to have, Ethiopian Abebe Bikila ran barefoot when he won the 1960 Rome Summer Olympic Marathon race in record time.

- 69 -

In 1990, women made up only 25% of road race finishers. Nowadays, more than half of race competitors are women.

- 70 -

The half marathon is the fastest growing race distance in the U.S. Since 2003, it has continued to double in participants each year. It has the most debut racers, finisher totals, and has the most interested racers due to its achievable distance. There are over 1500 active half marathons in the U.S.

- 71 -

Adult runners who played ball sports in their childhood and through youth have 50% fewer stress fractures than runners who didn't. That's because ball sports make bone mass greater and more symmetrically distributed. So, play football baseball, or soccer to increase your running performance.

- 7 2 -

The Kenyan tribe known as Kalenjin are notoriously incredibly fast runners. Of the top 20 distance runners in the world, 12 are its members. In addition to the mental training they go through as runners, their thin ankles and calves make them constantly successfully in almost every running-related sport.

- 7 3 -

If you find that you don't have enough breath to talk while you are running, you might be going too fast. Alternatively, if you find it easy to hold a conversation while running, you might want to up your speed and push yourself a bit harder.

- 7 4 -

Running strengthens your bones.

Your body accumulates more minerals in your leg bones to adapt to the effort of regular running. This increase in bone density gives professional runners thicker leg bone and structure than the average human being. It also makes their legs more resilient to the tiring effects of running. Research suggests that running 12-20 minutes three times per week is best for improving long-term bone stability and strength.

- 7 5 -

Excessive running could do more harm than good to your health.

This seems to counter the previous fact, but you can believe that it is true! Research shows that the effects of excessive long-term running can lead to bone damage and even respiratory illness. Those who ran over 80 km per week seemed to experience these issues in greater numbers than those that ran 20-50 km each week.

- 7 6 -

Runners store extra energy in their body. It can be about 2000 calories worth of glycogen, which supplies enough power and energy to run 18-20 miles.

- 7 7 -

People who run 20-30 km (12.4-18.6 miles) a week have a stronger immune system and are less prone to colds or infections. They are also 2x less likely to suffer from a respiratory illness than those who overtrain themselves.

- 7 8 -

Running improves cognitive abilities, concentration, focus, and memory. It's also powerful in waking creativity and getting fresh ideas. So, if you want a workout for your brain, go running.

- 7 9 -

Injuries can happen.

Although running brings numerous benefits, it is like every other physical sport on the planet and not without its risks. The most common injury runners face is PFPS or patellofemoral pain syndrome. "Runner's Knee", as it is generally referred to as, is a condition in which the cartilage under the kneecap becomes irritated. Other injuries that can occur in runners are muscle pain, ankle sprains, stress fractures, plantar fasciitis, shin splints, and Achilles tendonitis.

- 8 0 -

Keeping a regular running routine is the best way to enjoy the many benefits of running.

Preventing injuries, staying healthy, and living better with running happen best when you develop and stick to a running routine. If you don't have the time to run on a particular day, its best to still engage in some kind of physical activity to keep your mind and body in peak running shape.

- 8 1 -

The right shoes make all of the difference when it comes to running.

Running in shoes that don't fit right, or are in poor condition, can cause many problems when running. In addition to blisters and muscle pain, poor quality shoes can also cause bleeding and discoloration in the toenails.

- 8 2 -

Have you noticed that you often need a tissue while running? A runny nose is an annoying phenomenon which happens to most of the people who run outdoors. This is because cold and dry air increases nasal mucus production.

- 8 3 -

Those who run regularly live longer than those who don't run at all.

- 8 4 -

Running regularly has great effects on a person's mood, sleep quality, memory, and concentration levels.

- 8 5 -

Running helps you prevent cataracts, which is the leading cause of age-related vision problems, loss, and blindness. If you run an average of 5 miles (8 km) or more per day, you have a 41% lower risk of developing cataracts later in life. Your eyes will be grateful.

- 8 6 -

Running strengthens your heart and makes it pump blood throughout the body more efficiently. That makes your blood richer in oxygen with every heartbeat. This oxygenated blood is a real treasure for the whole body!

- 8 7 -

Running can prevent Alzheimer's disease. Although science doesn't know yet what exactly causes the progressive loss of memory, it's known for sure how you can prevent it. Our mind and spirit stay healthy in a healthy and robust body. Running improves our learning capacity and memory and also keeps our brain young. People who run regularly during their lifetime have significantly fewer chances to suffer from dementia in their old age.

- 8 8 -

According to studies, running makes you more desirable to others. In fact, 80% of men and 60% of women actually felt more attractive due to regular running. The physical health benefits of running make your body look and feel healthy which makes you more attractive to others. This increase in muscle tone and decrease in weight can have a positive impact on your social and personal relationships with others.

- 8 9 -

"Someone who is busier than you is running right now." This is a slogan from a Nike commercial, but it's entirely true! No matter how busy you are, you can always find a little time for running!

- 9 0 -

They say that long distance running is 10 percent body and 90 percent mind. It is important to train both your mind and body to get the best results from running long distances.

- 9 1 -

Running releases sweat, stress, and negative energy.

It makes you feel refreshed, positive, and relaxed.

- 9 2 -

"Every day is a good day when you run." No matter what the day brings, your daily run will be worth it. Taking time for yourself each day is important to putting your best self out into the world!

- 9 3 -

It's not always easy, but it's worth it. A few hours after running you will be glad that you did it. After a few weeks, you will be thrilled that you didn't give up, no matter how hard it was to start. In a few years, you won't even believe how you ever got through life without running.

- 9 4 -

There are some really old people running. The oldest marathon runner was 101 years old. Age is no excuse to not start running. Many runners began to run in their 40's, 50's, and even 70's!

- 9 5 -

You can run even with a baby in a stroller. If you are a busy mom, you still can run. Running with a stroller burns even more calories than usual running. And if a mom with a baby can do it, you can do it too! Stop making excuses and get back into the great shape you were in before you had a baby!

- 9 6 -

For only an hour a day, you can feel healthy, strong, and energetic!

- 9 7 -

Your favorite celebrities love to run! They include Pamela Anderson, George W. Bush, Oprah Winfrey, and Ryan Reynolds.

- 9 8 -

Finally get the incredible figure you want!

Running is one of the best ways to achieve the body you want to make yourself feel attractive and vibrant!

-99-

Change how you think about food! A lot of people struggle with overeating and late-night snacking. When you add running into your everyday activities, you don't have to feel guilty anymore because you will be burning off those extra calories in no time!

-100-

You'll get more years to enjoy life.

Runners live approximately seven years longer than those who don't run. That practically means seven more years for everything you love!

-101-

You need only 12-20 weeks to prepare for a marathon. That's not a huge time investment to start getting the long-lasting benefits that running provides!

12 TIPS FOR NEWBIE RUNNERS

~ 1 ~

Choose the right running shoes.

Running in supportive sneakers will make running more comfortable and lower the risk of injury to yourself. There are a variety of sneakers depending on sports activity, the kind of terrain, the mileage per week. If you don't know what shoes to choose, visit your local sports store to get help finding the right pair for you!

~ 2 ~

Start with realistic expectations.

Your first runs may be hard, and you might even reconsider this whole "running thing." No matter how hard it feels, it is important to not give up and stick to your goals. After a few weeks, the benefits you feel will allow you to set higher goals to reach and exceed in running.

~ 3 ~

To make running easy, start with short steps and running intervals.

Running demands a special technique. You'll need to learn it. Many beginners waste a lot of energy that makes running harder than it actually is. When you start running the first few times, try to take short and easy steps instead of big strides as they can slow you down. Also, as a newbie runner, don't plan to run the entire distance in one go. Break it up into smaller intervals and focus on completing them. Don't be ashamed to alternate them with walking to give yourself a little rest in between sets.

~ 4 ~

Don't worry about your pace or mileage. It is better to focus on consistency to make running a habit.

Don't pay attention to your speed or length of the distance you want to run. Focus instead on getting out for a run a few times a week. When you do it regularly for a few weeks, you'll be surprised how everything becomes easier. After you build your habit, you can move onto improving your pace and mileage.

~ 5 ~

Walk. A. Lot.

If you are new to running, you'll to need rest during each running session. Take short walk breaks whenever you need them. You can also alternate two minutes of running with two minutes of walking throughout the run.

~ 6 ~

Set small goals.

There's no reason to think you'll just get out there and run for 30 minutes without breaks or aches. Be realistic and set small goals. In the beginning, appropriate goals would be to make running a habit, perfect your running form, and work on breath control while running.

~ 7 ~

Do some warm-up exercises instead of stretching before a run. That way you'll prepare the body for the run without making it tired. You will also lower your chances of getting injured.

~ 8 ~

Increase mileage gradually.

Listen to what your body is telling you. You'll know when you're ready for a long distance when your current range is not challenging you anymore.

~ 9 ~

Keep a running journal.

Keeping track of your running times and distances on paper or through an app is a great way to keep track of the progress you are making. From these notes, you can set new running goals when your body is ready to handle them.

~ 10 ~

Take care of your body! Get good rest, eat properly, and drink enough water.

Running is a workout for the whole body. You need to use all of your muscles when running. your body should be well fed and energized so that you have all the power you need to finish your run. You can even include regular strength training to increase your running performance.

Don't forget that your body also needs time to recover. Alternate running days with rest when you first start running to give yourself time to heal and build strength. With the right balance of nutrients, minerals, proteins, fats, carbs, and water, you will have all you need to keep yourself in peak physical running shape.

~ 11 ~

Cross train and do a little bit of strength training.

It's good for your heart, joints, and spine. Alternating running with swimming, bike riding, or yoga is a great way to keep yourself in shape and not get bored with running.

~ 12 ~

Make a playlist or choose a podcast.

Most of the runners couldn't imagine running without their favorite music. If that sounds natural to you, make your playlist and enjoy. For those new to running, music can often be a distraction. If you find this is the case for you, consider switching to a podcast or audiobook until you have the mental focus you need to run to music.

CONCLUSION

We hope that you had fun reading all 101 Unbelievable Facts About Running!

Hopefully, these crazy, amusing, and unexpected facts have given you the motivation you need to get up and run!

For those considering picking up running, we hope our 12 Tips For Newbie Runners gives you everything you need to find the perfect sneakers, best routine, and awesome inspirations for making running your new favorite activity!

Remember, we are all born runners! While some of us have trained our body to be better at it than others, doing so is not impossible! It just requires a positive mental attitude, the right balance of nutrition, and the desire to feel good about yourself!

As the famous Nike slogan says, **"Just. Do. It."**